Name

Draw a Picture

I Can...

☐ use a Capital Letter
The cat is big.

☐ use spaces

☐ sound out words
d-o-g = dog

☐ use a Period .

☐ Draw a picture

He is having fun, running under the sun with his new toy gun.

fun	gun	run	sun
godere	pistola	correre	sole

Name: ______________________ Date: ______________________

Today is: Monday Tuesday Wednesday Thursday Friday

Direction: Trace and read the sentences.

bag	rag	tag	wag

sacchetto	straccio	etichetta	scodinzolante

He has many bags.

I see a rag.

I see a tag.

Its tail is wagging.

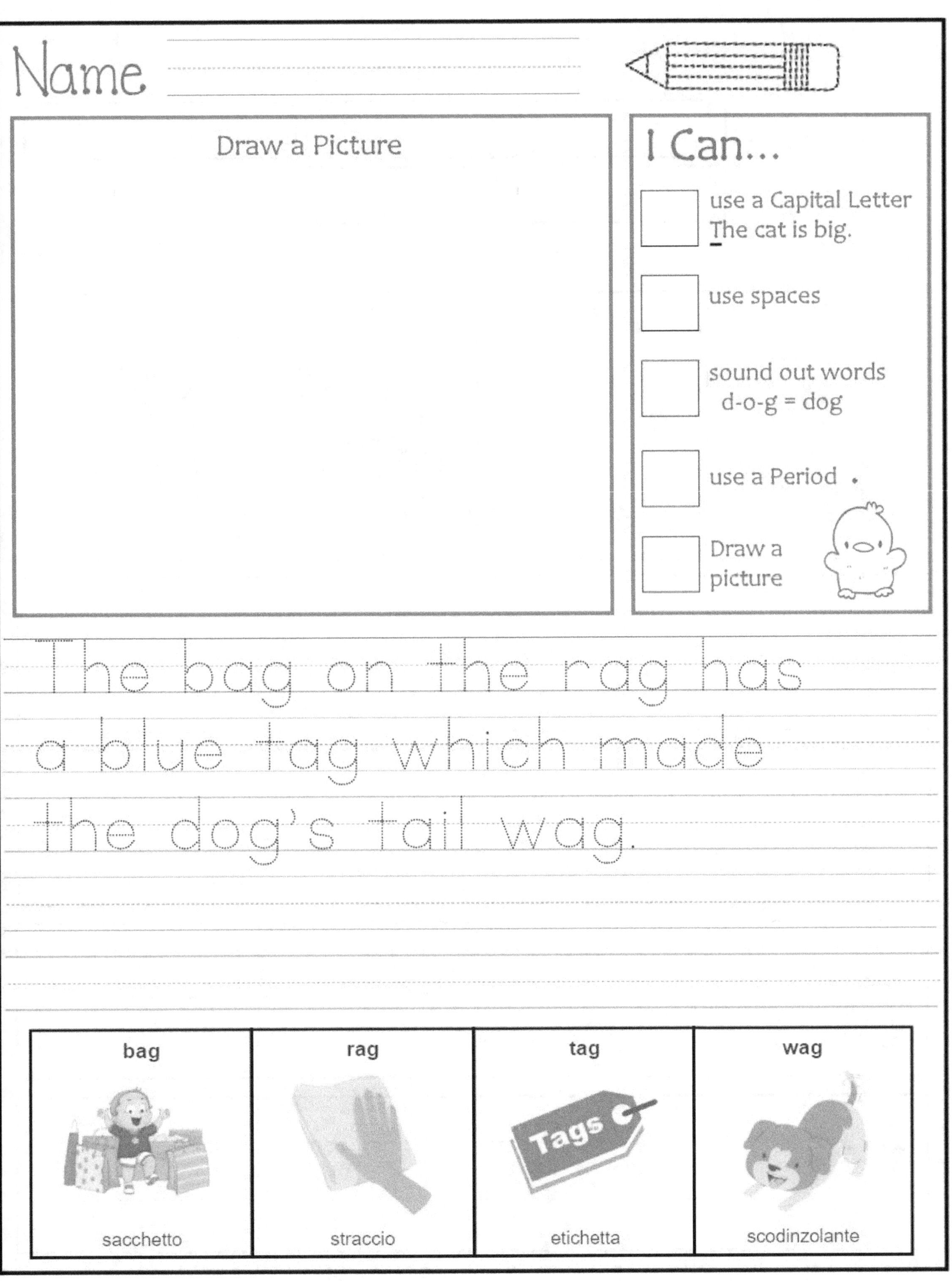

Name
Draw a Picture
I Can...
use a Capital Letter
The cat is big.
use spaces
sound out words
d-o-g = dog
use a Period .
Draw a picture
The bag on the rag has a blue tag which made the dog's tail wag.
bag
sacchetto
rag
straccio
tag
etichetta
wag
scodinzolante

Name: _______________ Date: _______________

Today is: Monday Tuesday Wednesday Thursday Friday

Direction: Trace and read the sentences.

can	man	pan	van
lattine	uomo	padella	furgone

I see a can of soda.

The man is happy.

The pan is dirty.

I see a big van.

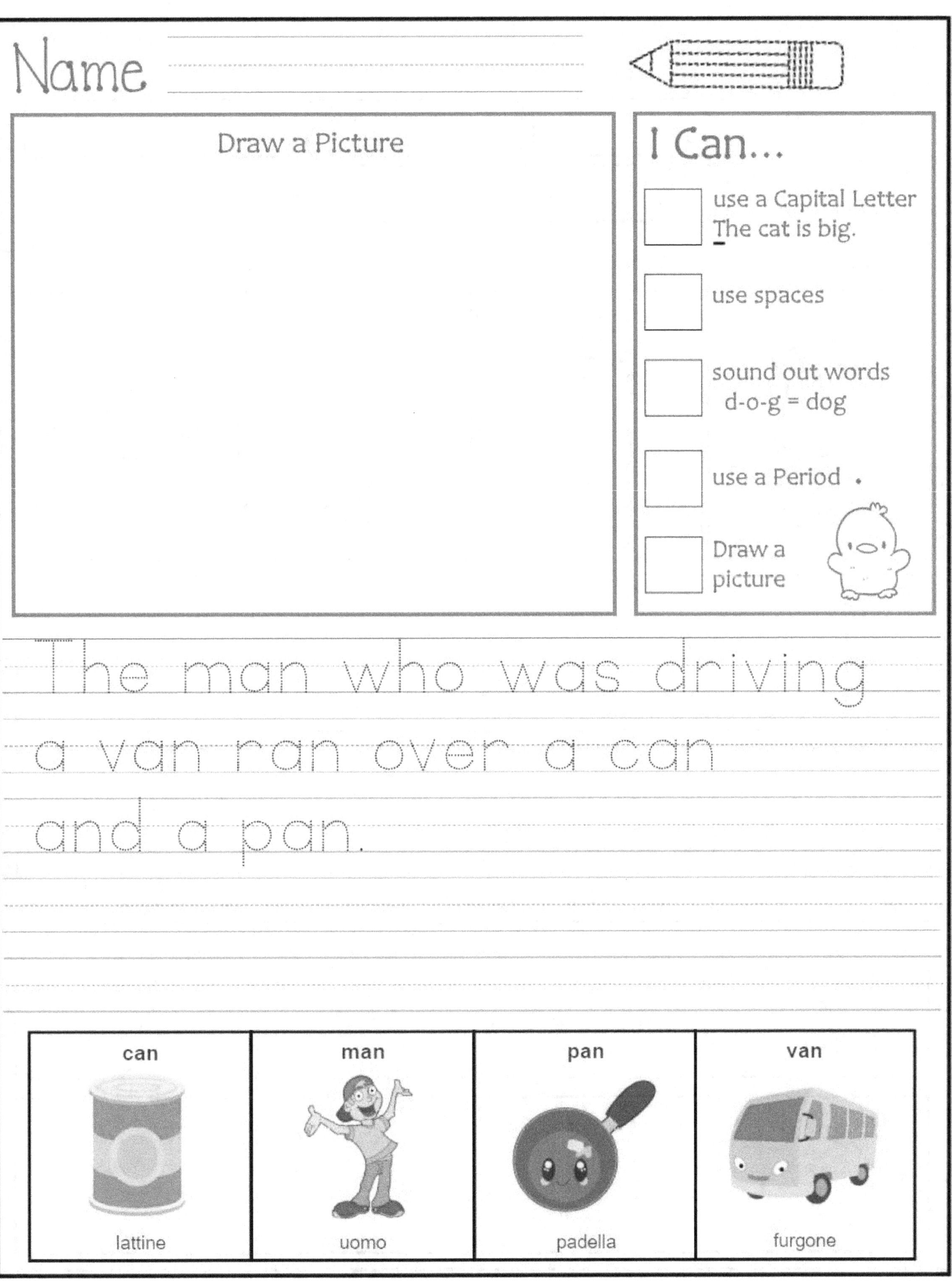

Name

Draw a Picture

I Can...

use a Capital Letter
The cat is big.

use spaces

sound out words
d-o-g = dog

use a Period .

Draw a
picture

The man who was driving
a van ran over a can
and a pan.

can
lattine

man
uomo

pan
padella

van
furgone

Name: _________________________ Date: _______________

Today is: [Monday] [Tuesday] [Wednesday]
[Thursday] [Friday]

Direction: Trace and read the sentences.

cut	**gut**	**hut**	**nut**
taglio	intestino	capanna	noce

He cut his nails.

He has a gut.

This is a small hut.

It is holding a nut.

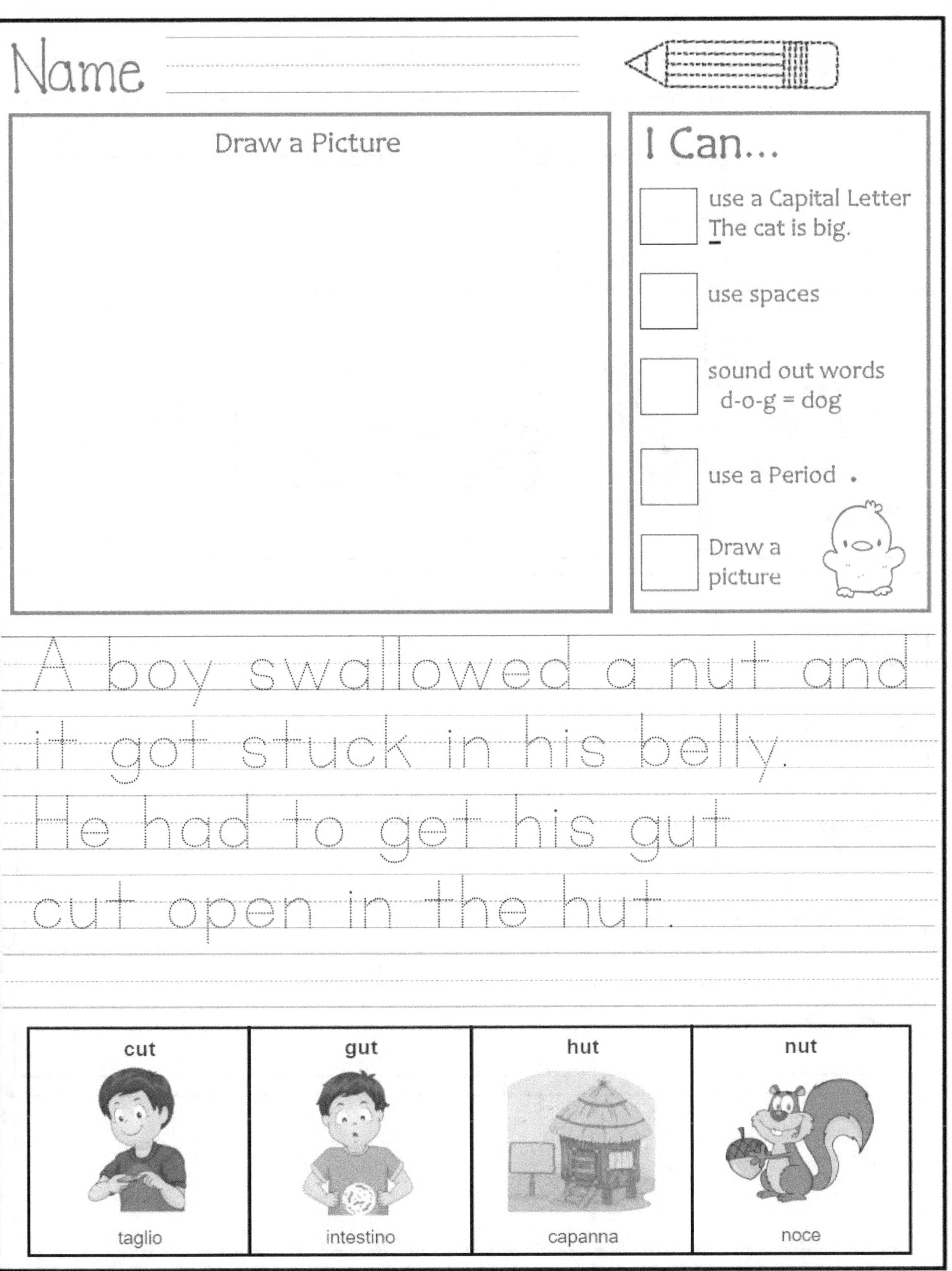
Name

Draw a Picture

I Can...

use a Capital Letter
The cat is big.

use spaces

sound out words
d-o-g = dog

use a Period .

Draw a
picture

A boy swallowed a nut and
it got stuck in his belly.
He had to get his gut
cut open in the hut.

cut
taglio

gut
intestino

hut
capanna

nut
noce

Name: ___________________ Date: ___________

Today is: Monday Tuesday Wednesday
Thursday Friday

Direction: Trace and read the sentences.

fat	cat	hat	mat
grasso	gatto	cappello	stuoia

I see a fat dog.

This is my little cat.

I like this hat.

I see a big mat.

Draw a Picture

I Can...

- [ ] use a Capital Letter
  The cat is big.
- [ ] use spaces
- [ ] sound out words
  d-o-g = dog
- [ ] use a Period .
- [ ] Draw a picture

The fat cat laid on the mat that was a hat pattern.

fat	cat	hat	mat
grasso	gatto	cappello	stuoia

Name: ____________________ Date: ____________________

Today is: Monday Tuesday Wednesday Thursday Friday

Direction: Trace and read the sentences.

cab	lab	tab	crab

taxi	laboratorio	linguetta	granchio

The cab is fast.

The lab is exciting.

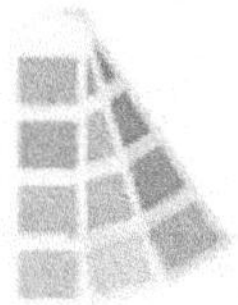

The tab is long.

We found a crab.

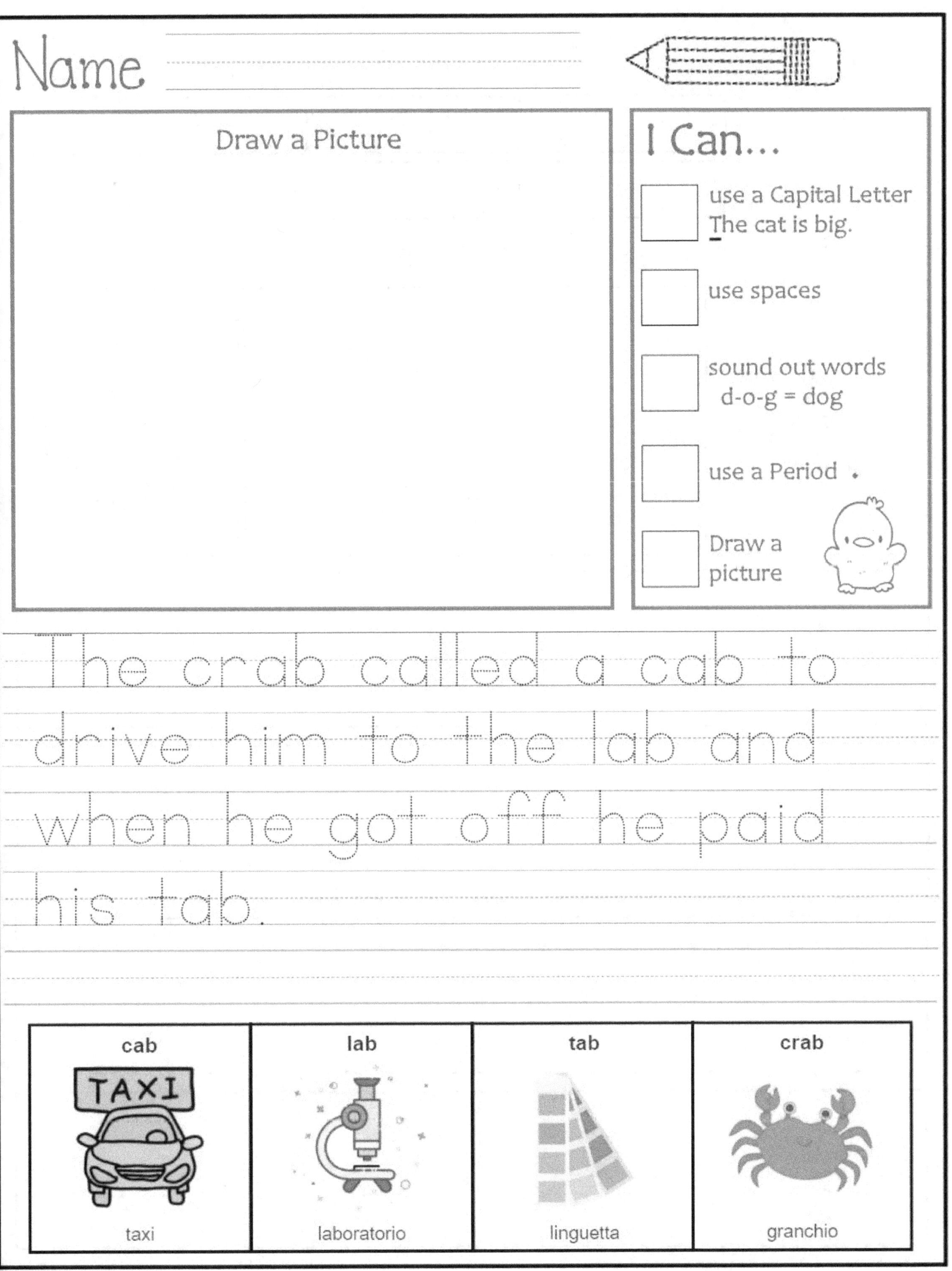
Name

Draw a Picture

I Can...

use a Capital Letter
The cat is big.

use spaces

sound out words
d-o-g = dog

use a Period .

Draw a
picture

The crab called a cab to
drive him to the lab and
when he got off he paid
his tab.

cab
TAXI
taxi

lab
laboratorio

tab
linguetta

crab
granchio

Name: ____________________ Date: ____________________

Today is: Monday Tuesday Wednesday Thursday Friday

Direction: Trace and read the sentences.

ham	jam	ram	clam
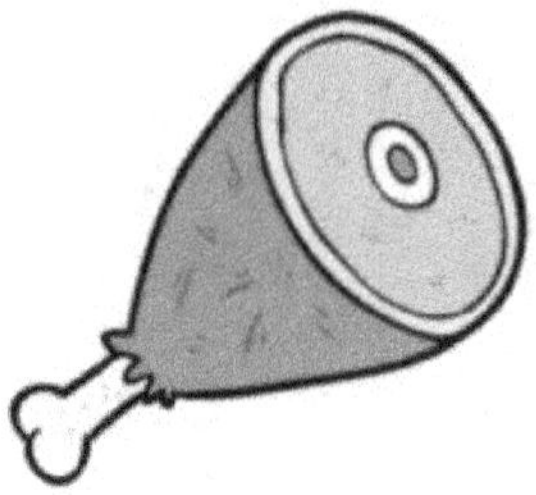	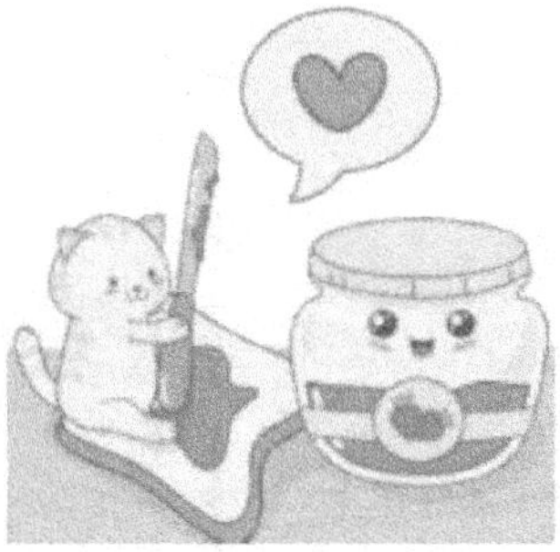	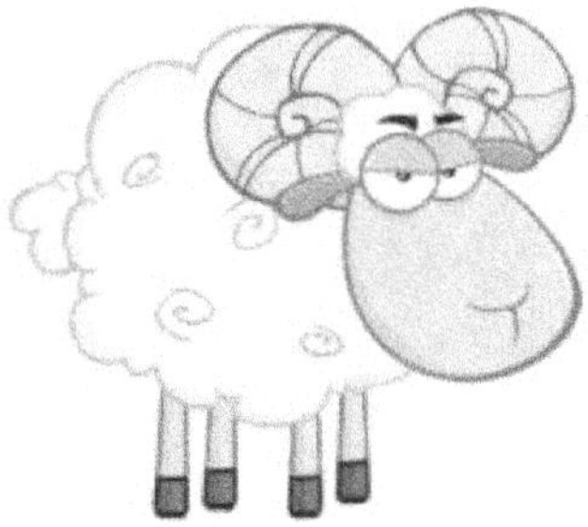	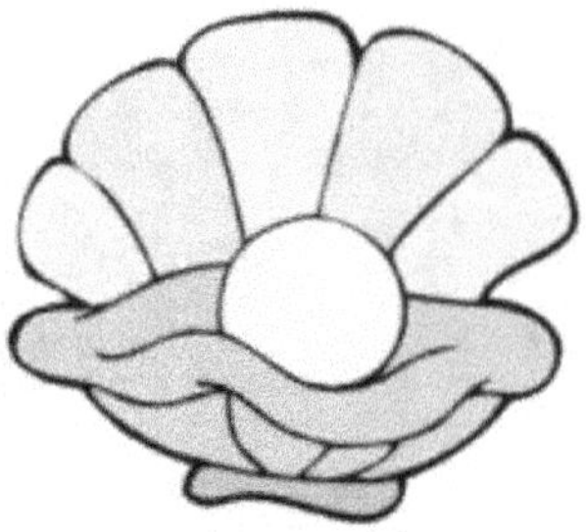
prosciutto	marmellata	pecora	mollusco

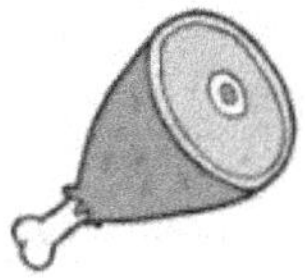
I like to eat ham.

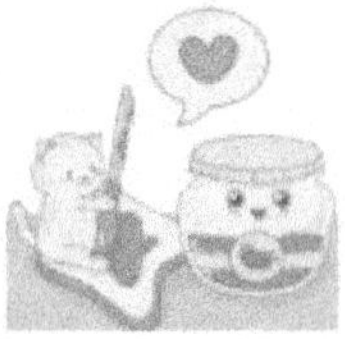
We like to eat jam.

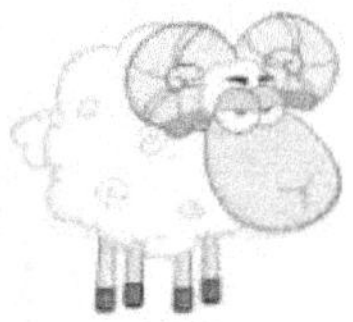
The ram is big.

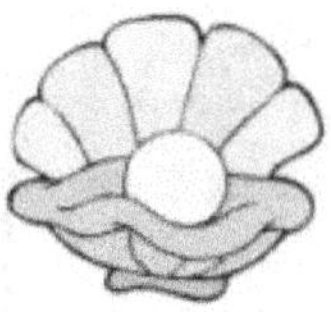
The clam is pretty.

Draw a Picture

I Can...

- [ ] use a Capital Letter
  The cat is big.
- [ ] use spaces
- [ ] sound out words
  d-o-g = dog
- [ ] use a Period .
- [ ] Draw a picture

The clam gave the ram ham. Then the ram gave the clam jam.

ham	jam	ram	clam
prosciutto	marmellata	pecora	mollusco

Name: _________________________ Date: _______________

Today is: [Monday] [Tuesday] [Wednesday]
[Thursday] [Friday]

Direction: Trace and read the sentences.

bed	**led**	**red**	**wed**
letto	principale	rosso	nozze

This is my little bed.

He led us to safety.

The apple is red.

He asks her to wed.

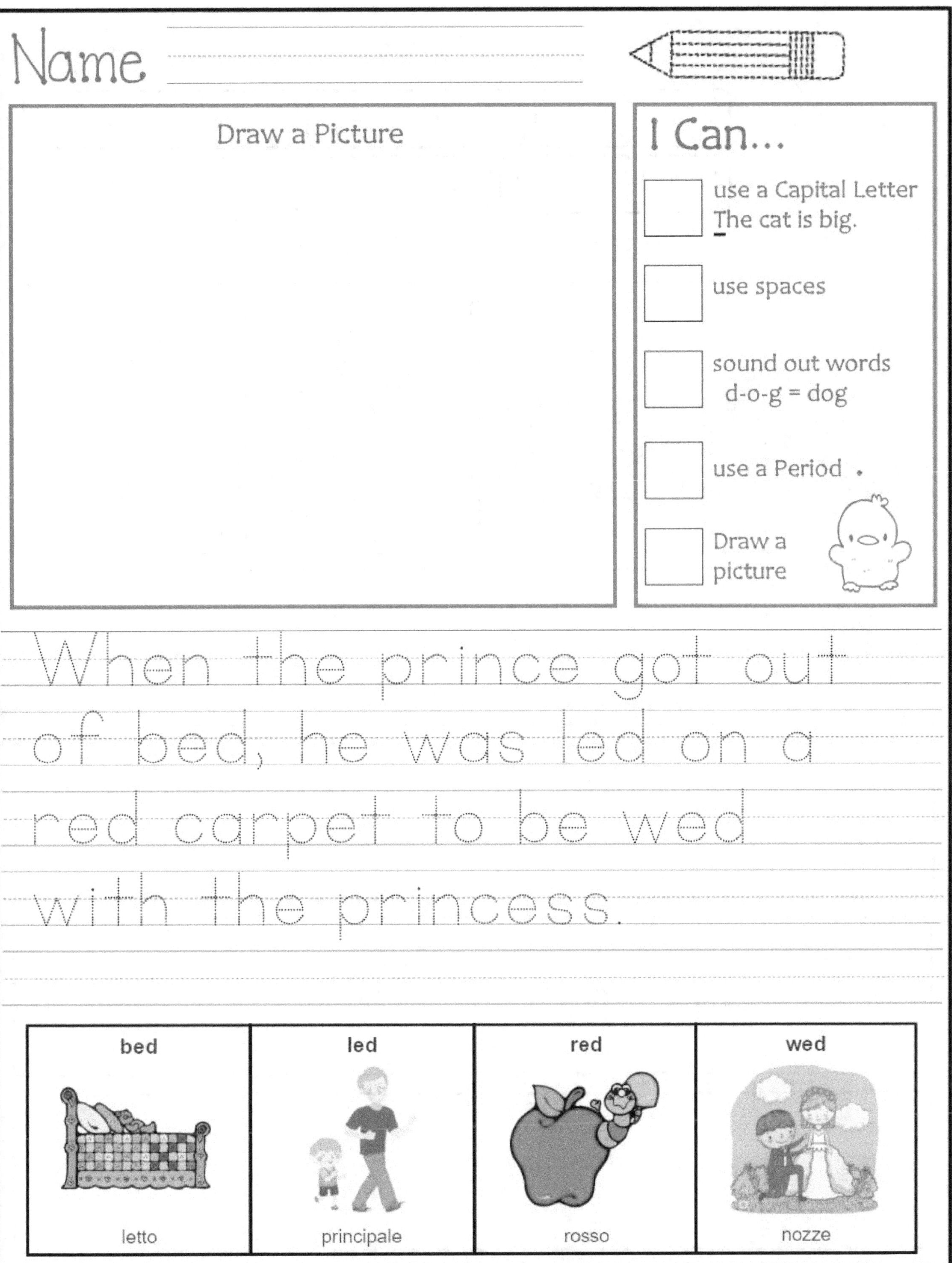

Name

Draw a Picture

I Can...

use a Capital Letter
The cat is big.

use spaces

sound out words
d-o-g = dog

use a Period .

Draw a
picture

When the prince got out of bed, he was led on a red carpet to be wed with the princess.

bed
letto

led
principale

red
rosso

wed
nozze

Name: ______________________ Date: ______________________

Today is: Monday Tuesday Wednesday Thursday Friday

Direction: Trace and read the sentences.

bad	dad	mad	sad

cattivo	papà	pazzo	triste

 This apple is bad.

 My dad is very kind.

 The reindeer is mad.

 The little cat is sad.

Draw a Picture

I Can...

- [ ] use a Capital Letter
  <u>T</u>he cat is big.
- [ ] use spaces
- [ ] sound out words
  d-o-g = dog
- [ ] use a Period .
- [ ] Draw a picture

I was bad so my dad
got mad and now
I am so sad.

bad	dad	mad	sad
cattivo	papà	pazzo	triste

Name: ___________________ Date: ___________

Today is: [Monday] [Tuesday] [Wednesday]
[Thursday] [Friday]

Direction: Trace and read the sentences.

den	**hen**	**pen**	**ten**
tana animale	gallina	stalle	dieci

It is a den.

The hens lay eggs.

She has a good pen.

The ten is smiling.

Draw a Picture

I Can...

- [ ] use a Capital Letter
  The cat is big.
- [ ] use spaces
- [ ] sound out words
  d-o-g = dog
- [ ] use a Period .
- [ ] Draw a picture

The hen that lived in the
pen laid ten eggs
in her den.

den	hen	pen	ten
tana animale	gallina	stalle	dieci

Name: _________________________ Date: _____________

Today is: Monday Tuesday Wednesday

Thursday Friday

Direction: Trace and read the sentences.

gum	mum	sum	drum
gommoso	mamma	somma	tamburo

I like to chew gum.

My mum is kind!

I can do a sum!

The drum is big.

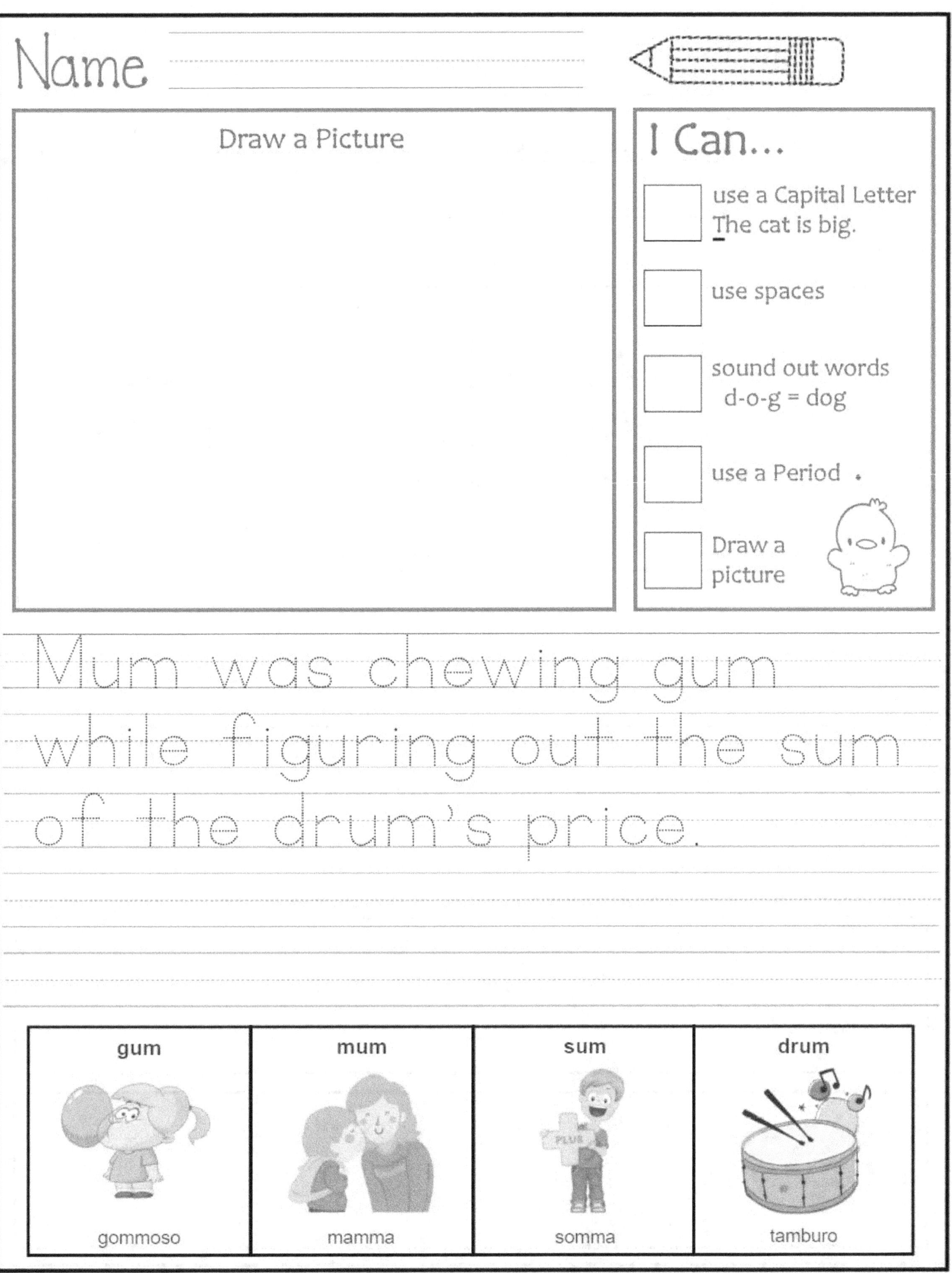

Name

Draw a Picture

I Can...

- [ ] use a Capital Letter
  <u>T</u>he cat is big.
- [ ] use spaces
- [ ] sound out words
  d-o-g = dog
- [ ] use a Period .
- [ ] Draw a picture

Mum was chewing gum while figuring out the sum of the drum's price.

gum	**mum**	**sum**	**drum**
gommoso	mamma	somma	tamburo

Name: _________________ Date: _________________

Today is: Monday Tuesday Wednesday Thursday Friday

Direction: Trace and read the sentences.

bid	hid	kid	lid
offerta	nascondere	ragazzo	coperchio

He likes to bid.

He is hiding.

The kid like to play.

I see a lid.

Draw a Picture

I Can...

- [ ] use a Capital Letter
  The cat is big.

- [ ] use spaces

- [ ] sound out words
  d-o-g = dog

- [ ] use a Period .

- [ ] Draw a picture

The kid bid a lid for one hundred dollars then hid from his mad parents.

bid	hid	kid	lid
offerta	nascondere	ragazzo	coperchio

Name: _________________________ Date: _______________

Today is: [Monday] [Tuesday] [Wednesday]
[Thursday] [Friday]

Direction: Trace and read the sentences.

big	**dig**	**pig**	**wig**
grande	scavare	maiale	parrucca

That is a big pencil.

He will dig up a hole.

The pig is fat.

She puts on a wig.

Draw a Picture

I Can...

- [ ] use a Capital Letter
  <u>T</u>he cat is big.

- [ ] use spaces

- [ ] sound out words
  d-o-g = dog

- [ ] use a Period .

- [ ] Draw a picture

The big pig went to dig in the mud for his wig.

big	dig	pig	wig
grande	scavare	maiale	parrucca

Name: _______________ Date: _______________

Today is: Monday Tuesday Wednesday

Thursday Friday

Direction: Trace and read the sentences.

bin	fin	pin	win
bidone	pinna	perno	vincere

It is a recycle bin.

The shark has a fin.

The pin is pointy.

He won the match.

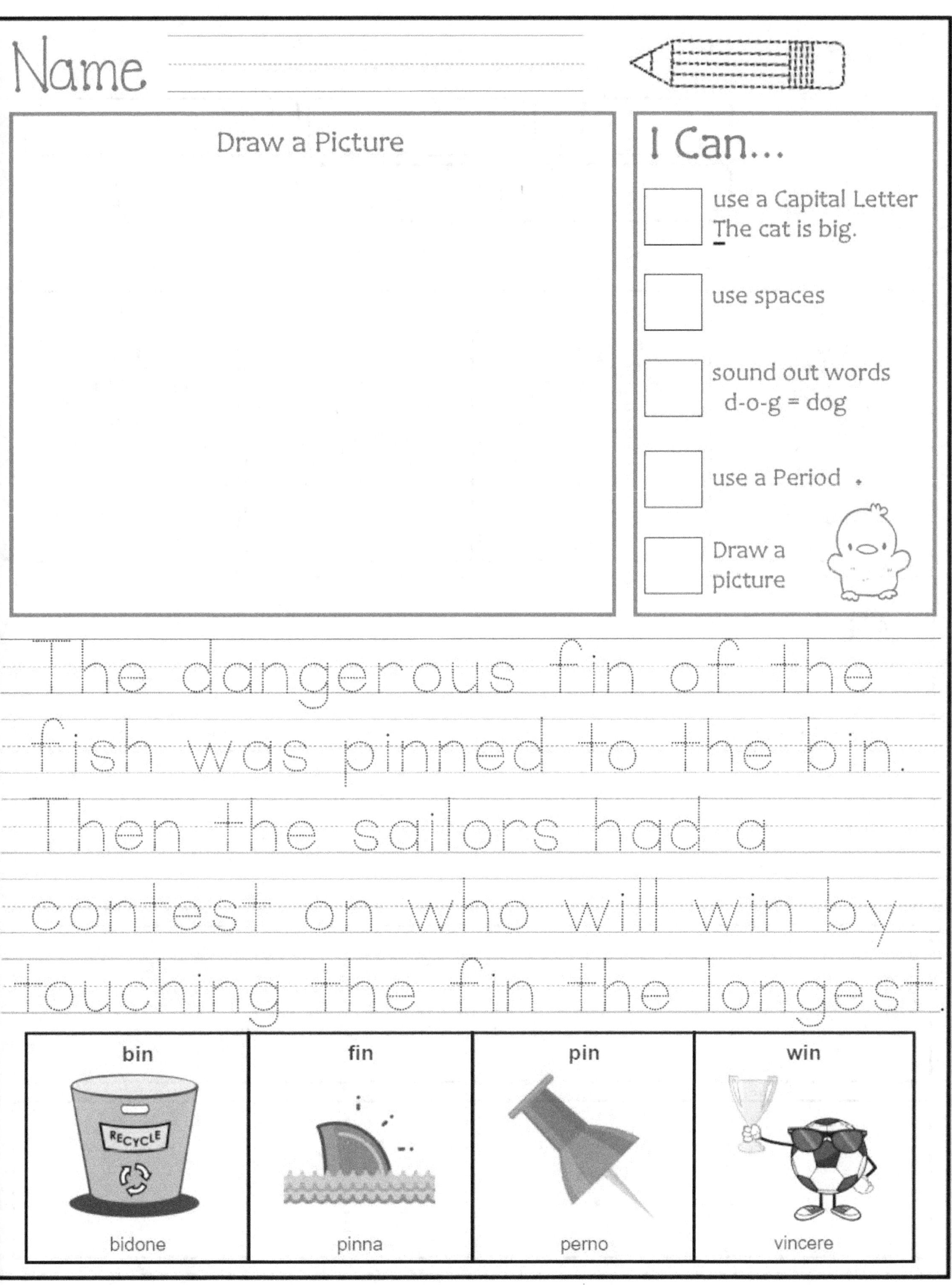

Name

Draw a Picture

I Can...
☐ use a Capital Letter
  The cat is big.
☐ use spaces
☐ sound out words
  d-o-g = dog
☐ use a Period .
☐ Draw a picture

The dangerous fin of the fish was pinned to the bin. Then the sailors had a contest on who will win by touching the fin the longest.

bin
RECYCLE
bidone

fin
pinna

pin
perno

win
vincere

Name: __________________ Date: __________

Today is: [Monday] [Tuesday] [Wednesday]
[Thursday] [Friday]

Direction: Trace and read the sentences.

hip	lip	nip	sip
anca	labbra	pizzicare	bevanda

This is my hip.

Her lips are red.

It is nipping its toy.

She is sipping.

Draw a Picture

I Can...

- use a Capital Letter
  The cat is big.
- use spaces
- sound out words
  d-o-g = dog
- use a Period .
- Draw a picture

The dog nipped someone who was sipping water with his lip.

hip	lip	nip	sip
anca	labbra	pizzicare	bevanda

Name: ______________________ Date: ______________________

Today is: [Monday] [Tuesday] [Wednesday] [Thursday] [Friday]

Direction: Trace and read the sentences.

fit	**hit**	**kit**	**sit**
in forma	colpire	kit	sedersi

It is perfectly fit.

They hit each other.

That is a safety kit.

He is sitting.

Draw a Picture

I Can...

- [ ] use a Capital Letter
  The cat is big.
- [ ] use spaces
- [ ] sound out words
  d-o-g = dog
- [ ] use a Period .
- [ ] Draw a picture

The fit doctor sat then was hit by a kit.

fit	hit	kit	sit
in forma	colpire	kit	sedersi

Name: ______________________ Date: ______________________

Today is: Monday Tuesday Wednesday Thursday Friday

Direction: Trace and read the sentences.

cob	job	rob	sob

mais	lavoro	rapinare	piangere

 I ate corn on the cob.

 This is my job.

 He is robbing.

 The girl is sobbing.

Draw a Picture

I Can...

- [ ] use a Capital Letter
  <u>T</u>he cat is big.
- [ ] use spaces
- [ ] sound out words
  d-o-g = dog
- [ ] use a Period .
- [ ] Draw a picture

The chef robbed a corn cob and then was sobbing because he had lost his job.

cob	job	rob	sob
mais	lavoro	rapinare	piangere

Name: ______________________ Date: ______________________

Today is: Monday Tuesday Wednesday Thursday Friday

Direction: Trace and read the sentences.

dog	hog	jog	log
			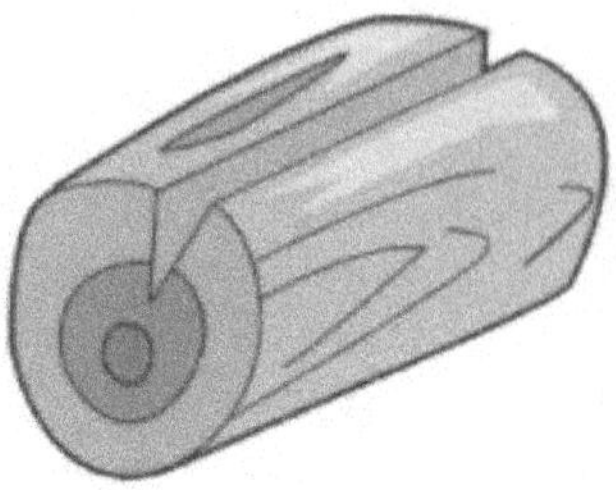
cane	maiale	jogging	legna

The dog is thrilled.

The hog is big.

She is jogging.

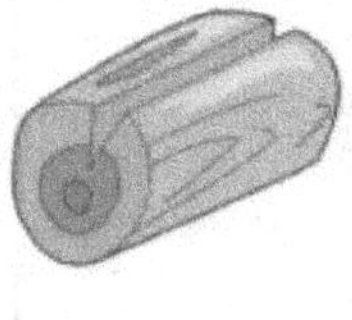

The log is small.

Name

Draw a Picture

I Can...

- [ ] use a Capital Letter
  The cat is big.

- [ ] use spaces

- [ ] sound out words
  d-o-g = dog

- [ ] use a Period .

- [ ] Draw a picture

The dog and the hog went for a jog but then tripped on a log.

dog	hog	jog	log
cane	maiale	jogging	legna

Name: _________________________ Date: _______________

Today is: [Monday] [Tuesday] [Wednesday]
[Thursday] [Friday]

Direction: Trace and read the sentences.

bug	hug	jug	mug
insetto	abbraccio	brocca	boccale

The bug is colorful.

She is hugging.

The jug has milk in it.

He has a mug.

Name

Draw a Picture

I Can...

use a Capital Letter
The cat is big.

use spaces

sound out words
d-o-g = dog

use a Period .

Draw a
picture

The bug hugged the jug
and the mug which was
full of jam.

bug
insetto

hug
abbraccio

jug
brocca

mug
boccale

Name: ____________________ Date: ____________________

Today is: Monday Tuesday Wednesday Thursday Friday

Direction: Trace and read the sentences.

cot	dot	hot	pot

letto	punto	caldo	pentola

 This is my cot.

 There are many dots.

 It is very hot.

 He has a plant pot.

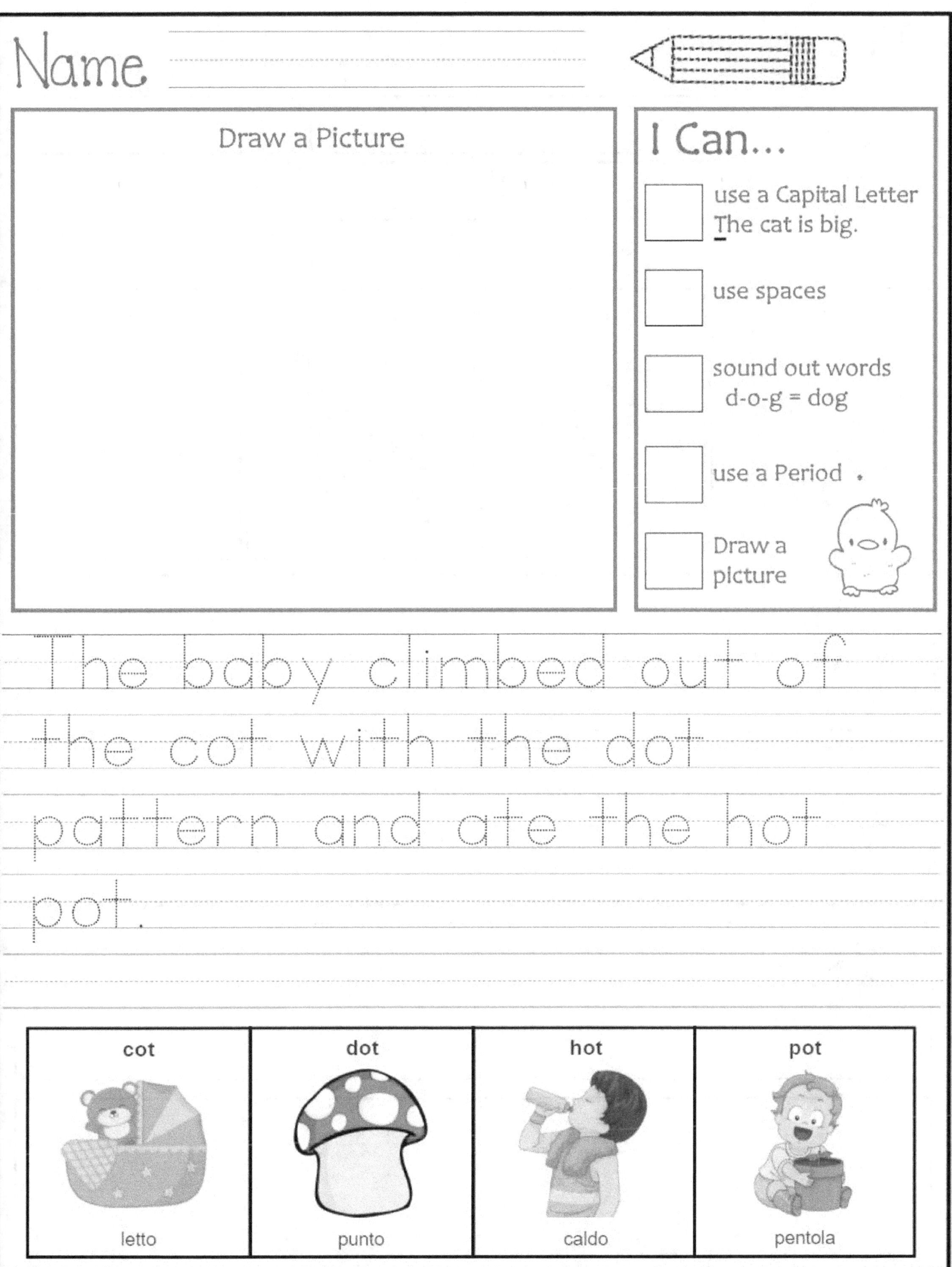

Name

Draw a Picture

I Can...

- [ ] use a Capital Letter
  <u>T</u>he cat is big.
- [ ] use spaces
- [ ] sound out words
  d-o-g = dog
- [ ] use a Period .
- [ ] Draw a picture

The baby climbed out of the cot with the dot pattern and ate the hot pot.

cot	dot	hot	pot
letto	punto	caldo	pentola

Name: _______________________ Date: _______________

Today is: | Monday | Tuesday | Wednesday |
           | Thursday | Friday |

Direction: Read the words and make a sentence.

fun	**gun**	**run**	**sun**
godere	pistola	correre	sole

Name

Draw a Picture

I Can...

- [ ] use a Capital Letter
  <u>T</u>he cat is big.

- [ ] use spaces

- [ ] sound out words
  d-o-g = dog

- [ ] use a Period .

- [ ] Draw a picture

Name: _______________________ Date: _______________

Today is: Monday Tuesday Wednesday Thursday Friday

Name: _________________ Date: _______________

Today is: [Monday] [Tuesday] [Wednesday]
[Thursday] [Friday]

Direction: Read the words and make a sentence.

bag	**rag**	**tag**	**wag**
sacchetto	straccio	etichetta	scodinzolante

Name _______________________

Draw a Picture

I Can...

- [ ] use a Capital Letter
  <u>T</u>he cat is big.

- [ ] use spaces

- [ ] sound out words
  d-o-g = dog

- [ ] use a Period .

- [ ] Draw a picture

Name: _______________________ Date: _______

Today is: Monday Tuesday Wednesday
          Thursday Friday

Name: _______________ Date: _______________

Today is: [Monday] [Tuesday] [Wednesday]
[Thursday] [Friday]

Direction: Read the words and make a sentence.

can	man	pan	van
lattine	uomo	padella	furgone

Name

Draw a Picture

I Can...

☐ use a Capital Letter
The cat is big.

☐ use spaces

☐ sound out words
d-o-g = dog

☐ use a Period .

☐ Draw a picture

Name: _______________________ Date: _______________

Today is: Monday Tuesday Wednesday Thursday Friday

Name: _________________________ Date: _____________________

Today is: [Monday] [Tuesday] [Wednesday]
[Thursday] [Friday]

Direction: Read the words and make a sentence.

cut	**gut**	**hut**	**nut**
taglio	intestino	capanna	noce

<u>Name</u>

Draw a Picture

I Can...

☐ use a Capital Letter
<u>T</u>he cat is big.

☐ use spaces

☐ sound out words
d-o-g = dog

☐ use a Period .

☐ Draw a picture

Name: _______________________ Date: _______________

Today is: [Monday] [Tuesday] [Wednesday]
[Thursday] [Friday]

Name: _______________________ Date: _______________________

Today is: Monday Tuesday Wednesday Thursday Friday

Direction: Read the words and make a sentence.

fat	cat	hat	mat
grasso	gatto	cappello	stuoia

Name ____________________________

Draw a Picture

I Can...

- [ ] use a Capital Letter
  The cat is big.

- [ ] use spaces

- [ ] sound out words
  d-o-g = dog

- [ ] use a Period .

- [ ] Draw a picture

Name: _______________________ Date: _______________

Today is: Monday Tuesday Wednesday Thursday Friday

Name: _________________________ Date: _________________

Today is: Monday Tuesday Wednesday Thursday Friday

Direction: Read the words and make a sentence.

cab	lab	tab	crab
taxi	laboratorio	linguetta	granchio

Name

Draw a Picture

I Can...

- [ ] use a Capital Letter
  <u>T</u>he cat is big.

- [ ] use spaces

- [ ] sound out words
  d-o-g = dog

- [ ] use a Period .

- [ ] Draw a picture

Name: ___________________________ Date: ___________

Today is: Monday Tuesday Wednesday Thursday Friday

Name: _______________________ Date: _______________________

Today is:
Monday Tuesday Wednesday
Thursday Friday

Direction: Read the words and make a sentence.

ham	jam	ram	clam
prosciutto	marmellata	pecora	mollusco

Name

Draw a Picture

I Can...

- [ ] use a Capital Letter
  The cat is big.

- [ ] use spaces

- [ ] sound out words
  d-o-g = dog

- [ ] use a Period .

- [ ] Draw a picture

Name: _______________________   Date: _______________

Today is: [Monday] [Tuesday] [Wednesday]
           [Thursday] [Friday]

Name: _______________________ Date: _______________________

Today is: Monday Tuesday Wednesday Thursday Friday

Direction: Read the words and make a sentence.

bed	**led**	**red**	**wed**
letto	principale	rosso	nozze

Name

Draw a Picture

I Can...

- [ ] use a Capital Letter
  The cat is big.

- [ ] use spaces

- [ ] sound out words
  d-o-g = dog

- [ ] use a Period .

- [ ] Draw a picture

Name: _______________________ Date: _______________________

Today is: Monday | Tuesday | Wednesday | Thursday | Friday

Name: _________________ Date: _________________

Today is: Monday Tuesday Wednesday Thursday Friday

Direction: Read the words and make a sentence.

bad	**dad**	**mad**	**sad**
cattivo	papà	pazzo	triste

Name

Draw a Picture

I Can...

- [ ] use a Capital Letter
  <u>T</u>he cat is big.

- [ ] use spaces

- [ ] sound out words
  d-o-g = dog

- [ ] use a Period .

- [ ] Draw a picture

Name: _______________________ Date: _______________________

Today is: Monday Tuesday Wednesday Thursday Friday

Name: _________________________ Date: _________________

Today is: [Monday] [Tuesday] [Wednesday]
[Thursday] [Friday]

Direction: Read the words and make a sentence.

den	**hen**	**pen**	**ten**
tana animale	gallina	stalle	dieci

Name

Draw a Picture

I Can...

- [ ] use a Capital Letter
  <u>T</u>he cat is big.

- [ ] use spaces

- [ ] sound out words
  d-o-g = dog

- [ ] use a Period .

- [ ] Draw a picture

Name: _______________________ Date: _______________

Today is: Monday | Tuesday | Wednesday
Thursday | Friday

Name: _________________________ Date: _______________

Today is: [Monday] [Tuesday] [Wednesday]
[Thursday] [Friday]

Direction: Read the words and make a sentence.

gum	**mum**	**sum**	**drum**
gommoso	mamma	somma	tamburo

Name

Draw a Picture

I Can...

☐ use a Capital Letter
  <u>T</u>he cat is big.

☐ use spaces

☐ sound out words
  d-o-g = dog

☐ use a Period .

☐ Draw a picture

Name: _______________________ Date: _______________________

Today is: Monday Tuesday Wednesday Thursday Friday

Name: _______________________ Date: _______________

Today is: Monday Tuesday Wednesday
Thursday Friday

Direction: Read the words and make a sentence.

bid	hid	kid	lid
offerta	nascondere	ragazzo	coperchio

Name

Draw a Picture

I Can...

☐ use a Capital Letter
The cat is big.

☐ use spaces

☐ sound out words
d-o-g = dog

☐ use a Period .

☐ Draw a picture

Name: ___________________ Date: ___________

Today is: Monday Tuesday Wednesday

Thursday Friday

Name: _______________ Date: _______________

Today is: Monday Tuesday Wednesday

Thursday Friday

Direction: Read the words and make a sentence.

big	dig	pig	wig
grande	scavare	maiale	parrucca

Name

Draw a Picture

I Can...

- [ ] use a Capital Letter
  The cat is big.

- [ ] use spaces

- [ ] sound out words
  d-o-g = dog

- [ ] use a Period .

- [ ] Draw a picture

Name: _________________ Date: _________

Today is: Monday Tuesday Wednesday Thursday Friday

Name: _____________________ Date: _____________

Today is: | Monday | Tuesday | Wednesday |
| Thursday | Friday |

Direction: Read the words and make a sentence.

| **bin** | **fin** | **pin** | **win** |
| bidone | pinna | perno | vincere |

Name

Draw a Picture

I Can...

☐ use a Capital Letter
  <u>T</u>he cat is big.

☐ use spaces

☐ sound out words
  d-o-g = dog

☐ use a Period .

☐ Draw a picture

Name: _______________________ Date: _______________

Today is: [Monday] [Tuesday] [Wednesday]
[Thursday] [Friday]

Name: ______________________ Date: ______________________

Today is: Monday Tuesday Wednesday Thursday Friday

Direction: Read the words and make a sentence.

hip	lip	nip	sip
anca	labbra	pizzicare	bevanda

Name

Draw a Picture

I Can...

- [ ] use a Capital Letter
  The cat is big.

- [ ] use spaces

- [ ] sound out words
  d-o-g = dog

- [ ] use a Period .

- [ ] Draw a picture

Name: _____________________ Date: _____________

Today is: [Monday] [Tuesday] [Wednesday] [Thursday] [Friday]

Name: _______________________ Date: _______________

Today is: Monday Tuesday Wednesday

Thursday Friday

Direction: Read the words and make a sentence.

fit	**hit**	**kit**	**sit**
in forma	colpire	kit	sedersi

Name

Draw a Picture

I Can...

☐ use a Capital Letter
<u>T</u>he cat is big.

☐ use spaces

☐ sound out words
d-o-g = dog

☐ use a Period .

☐ Draw a
picture

Name: _______________________   Date: _______________

Today is: Monday   Tuesday   Wednesday   Thursday   Friday

Name: _______________________ Date: _______________

Today is: Monday   Tuesday   Wednesday
Thursday   Friday

Direction: Read the words and make a sentence.

cob	**job**	**rob**	**sob**
mais	lavoro	rapinare	piangere

Draw a Picture

I Can...

- [ ] use a Capital Letter
  The cat is big.

- [ ] use spaces

- [ ] sound out words
  d-o-g = dog

- [ ] use a Period .

- [ ] Draw a picture

Name: _________________________ Date: _______________

Today is: Monday Tuesday Wednesday
Thursday Friday

Name: _________________________ Date: _______________

Today is: [Monday] [Tuesday] [Wednesday]
[Thursday] [Friday]

Direction: Read the words and make a sentence.

| **dog** | **hog** | **jog** | **log** |
| cane | maiale | jogging | legna |

Name

Draw a Picture

I Can...

☐ use a Capital Letter
The cat is big.

☐ use spaces

☐ sound out words
d-o-g = dog

☐ use a Period .

☐ Draw a picture

Name: _________________________ Date: _________________________

Today is: | Monday | Tuesday | Wednesday |

Thursday | Friday |

bug	hug	jug	mug
insetto	abbraccio	brocca	boccale

Name

Draw a Picture

I Can...

- [ ] use a Capital Letter
  The cat is big.

- [ ] use spaces

- [ ] sound out words
  d-o-g = dog

- [ ] use a Period .

- [ ] Draw a picture

Name: _______________________ Date: _______________________

Today is: Monday Tuesday Wednesday Thursday Friday

Name: _________________ Date: _____________

Today is: [Monday] [Tuesday] [Wednesday]
[Thursday] [Friday]

Direction: Read the words and make a sentence.

cot	dot	hot	pot
letto	punto	caldo	pentola

Name

Draw a Picture

I Can...

- [ ] use a Capital Letter
  The cat is big.

- [ ] use spaces

- [ ] sound out words
  d-o-g = dog

- [ ] use a Period .

- [ ] Draw a picture

Name: _______________________   Date: _______________________

Today is: Monday   Tuesday   Wednesday
           Thursday   Friday